Bird orders

D1400478

Jungle fowl, grouse, quail, and relatives

Galliformes
300 species

Pigeons and doves

Columbiformes
343 species

Tinamous

Tinamiformes
47 species

Perching birds

Passeriformes
6,456 species

Hoatzin

Opisthocomiformes
1 species

Cuckoo roller

Leptosomiformes
1 species

Touracos

Musophagiformes
23 species

Albatrosses, petrels, and relatives

Procellariiformes
147 species

Cranes, rails, and relatives

Gruiformes
189 species

Cuckoos

Cuculiformes
26 species

Trogons and quetzals

Trogoniformes
43 species

Mesites

Mesitornithiformes
3 species

Kingfishers and relatives

Coraciiformes
177 species

Birds of prey

Accipitriformes
266 species

Colies

Coliiformes
6 species

Sandgrouse

Pterocliformes
16 species

Parrots

Psittaciformes
398 species

Emus and cassowaries

Casuariiformes
4 species

Owls

Strigiformes
243 species

Tropic birds

Phaethontiformes
3 species

Things to find out:

DK findout! Birds

ELKHART LAKE PUBLIC LIBRARY
40 Pine Street
P.O. Box 387
Elkhart Lake, WI 53020

Author: Ben Hoare
Consultant: Dr. Paul Gale

Senior editors Jolyon Goddard, Roohi Sehgal
Senior art editor Ann Cannings
Art editors Kanika Kalra, Mohd Zishan
US Senior editor Shannon Beatty
US Editor Elizabeth Searcy
DTP designers Sachin Gupta, Vikram Singh
Picture researcher Sakshi Saluja
Jacket coordinator Issy Walsh
Jacket designer Dheeraj Arora
Managing editors Laura Gilbert, Monica Saigal
Deputy managing art editor Ivy Sengupta
Managing art editor Diane Peyton Jones
Preproduction producer Heather Blagden
Producer John Casey
Delhi team head Malavika Talukder
Creative director Helen Senior
Publishing director Sarah Larter

Educational consultant Jenny Lane-Smith

First American Edition 2019
Published in the United States by DK Publishing
1450 Broadway, Suite 801, New York, NY 10018

Copyright © 2019 Dorling Kindersley Limited
DK, a Division of Penguin Random House LLC
19 20 21 22 23 10 9 8 7 6 5 4 3 2 1
001–311572–Jun/2019

All rights reserved. Without limiting the rights under
the copyright reserved above, no part of this publication may
be reproduced, stored in or introduced into a retrieval system,
or transmitted, in any form, or by any means (electronic,
mechanical, photocopying, recording, or otherwise), without
the prior written permission of the copyright owner.
Published in Great Britain by Dorling Kindersley Limited.

A catalog record for this book is available from
the Library of Congress.
ISBN: 978-1-4654-8151-1 (Flexibound)
ISBN: 978-1-4654-8152-8 (Hardcover)

DK books are available at special discounts when purchased in bulk
for sales promotions, premiums, fund-raising, or educational use.
For details, contact: DK Publishing Special Markets,
1450 Broadway, Suite 801, New York, NY 10018
SpecialSales@dk.com

Printed and bound in China

A WORLD OF IDEAS:
SEE ALL THERE IS TO KNOW
www.dk.com

Contents

The scale boxes on pages 44–57 of this book show you how big a bird is compared to a person who is 6 ft (1.8 m) tall or a hand that is 7 in (18 cm) high.

» Scale

» Scale

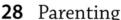

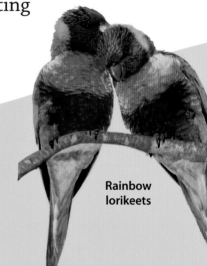

Rainbow lorikeets

Bald eagle

Sword-billed hummingbird

Mandarin duck

Eastern bluebird

Peafowl

What is a bird?

Birds come in many shapes and sizes, but there are some things they all share. All birds are vertebrates, which means they have a backbone. They all have a bill, wings, and scaly legs, and they lay eggs. Birds are the only animals with feathers. Feathers help them fly and provide warmth.

Eyes

Birds have big eyes and excellent eyesight. They often see much more detail than we do and can spot food from great heights. Such big eyes take up a large amount of space inside the head.

Bald eagle

Toco toucan

Boobook owl

Bill

A bird's bill is a tool for many jobs. It is used to clean and tidy feathers, build nests, and pick up food. Each bird has a differently shaped bill, suited to the type of food it eats.

Feet

Most birds have strong feet. They use their feet for perching on things, running, or swimming. Some birds also catch prey with their feet. They have between two and four toes, each ending in a sharp claw.

Blue-and-yellow macaw

Wings

Wings enable a bird to fly. They flap with great force to lift the bird off the ground. Once in the air, birds can flutter, glide, soar, hover, or dive, depending on their wing shape.

Evolution

Archaeopteryx (ar-kee-OP-ter-ix) is the earliest known bird. It lived about 150 million years ago in the Late Jurassic period. The size of a raven, Archaeopteryx evolved from dinosaurs that climbed trees. Like a bird, it had feathers and wings. However, like a dinosaur, it also had claws (on its wings) and teeth.

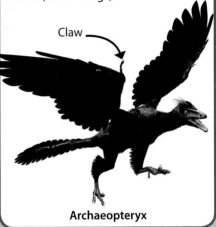

Claw

Archaeopteryx

! WOW!

There are about **10,700 different species**, or types, of bird in the world.

Golden pheasant

Swallow-tailed hummingbird

Body

Birds have light but strong skeletons with hollow bones. Most of a bird's body is covered with feathers, which weigh very little and keep the body warm and dry.

Tail

Birds use their tails to steer when flying and to brake when landing. The tail provides balance when they are perched on a branch or walking on the ground.

Body feathers
These feathers give birds a streamlined shape. They can have a huge range of colors.

Feathers

All birds have feathers. They grow out of the skin and are made of keratin. Keratin is a tough, lightweight substance that is also found in human nails and hair. There are different types of feathers. Some are used for flight, while others cover the body and keep birds warm.

Tail feathers
Long tail feathers are used to steer during flight, balance when perched, and show off to other birds.

Red-and-green macaw

Uses of feathers

Feathers are not just for flight. They also help birds show off to attract mates or look fierce. Feathers provide camouflage and protection, too.

Wing feathers
The stiff feathers on a bird's wings are essential for flight.

Pacific royal flycatcher

Display
Many male birds have bold feathers, such as this crest. They like to display, or show off, these feathers to impress females or scare away rivals and enemies.

Parts of a feather

Feathers have a shaft running down the middle of them. Its hollow end, which grows out of the bird's skin, is called a quill. Coming off the shaft are thin branches, called barbs. These in turn have even thinner branches, called barbules, which link up to create a smooth surface, or vane.

This closeup view shows how barbules zip together to form the vane.

Vane

Shaft

Quill

Camouflage
Birds often have feathers with colors that help them blend into the background. This camouflage can make them invisible to prey or predators.

Common potoo

Protection
Feathers protect birds from the cold. They trap a layer of warm air next to the body, keeping it cozy.

Snowy owl

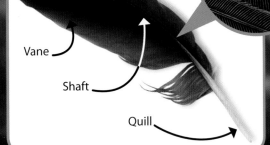

Flight

Only three types of animal can truly fly—insects, bats, and birds. Being very light for their size is the key to birds' success in the air. Their wings are powered by massive flight muscles. These help overcome the force of gravity and lift birds into the air, like the engines of an aircraft.

Wrist
The longest wing feathers spread out from the wrist. It is one of three joints in the wing.

Forearm
In a bird, the front two limbs have evolved into wings.

Skeleton

To weigh less for flight, a bird's bones are filled mostly with air. Having a bill helps too, because it weighs much less than jaws and teeth.

Tailbone
This bone supports the tail feathers, which fan out from here.

How does a bird fly?

To get airborne, a bird jumps up using its strong leg muscles. It then flaps its wings hard to push itself forward. Air passing over the wings produces lift.

Taking off
As this pigeon's wings rise, the feathers twist apart to allow air through.

Starting to flap
The pigeon lifts its wings up high, so they almost touch one another at the top.

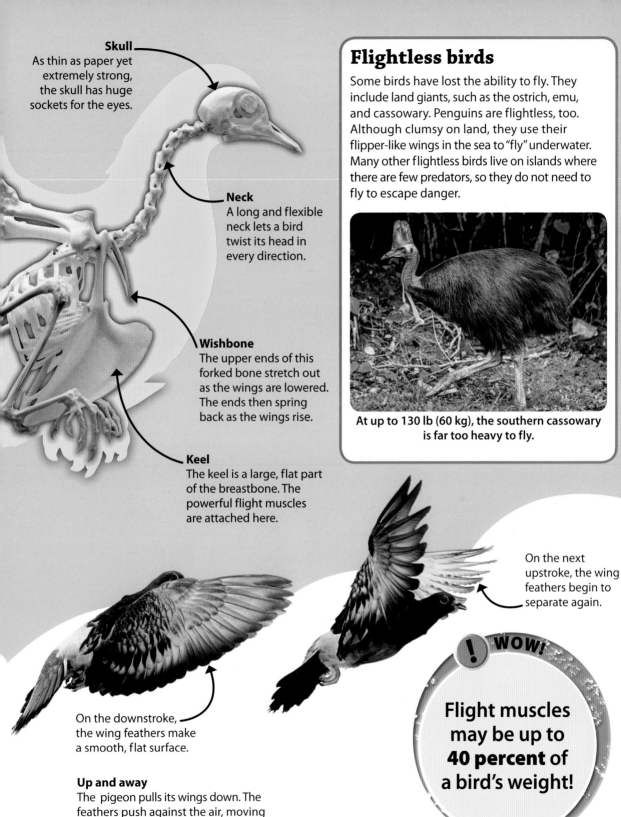

Skull
As thin as paper yet extremely strong, the skull has huge sockets for the eyes.

Neck
A long and flexible neck lets a bird twist its head in every direction.

Wishbone
The upper ends of this forked bone stretch out as the wings are lowered. The ends then spring back as the wings rise.

Keel
The keel is a large, flat part of the breastbone. The powerful flight muscles are attached here.

Flightless birds

Some birds have lost the ability to fly. They include land giants, such as the ostrich, emu, and cassowary. Penguins are flightless, too. Although clumsy on land, they use their flipper-like wings in the sea to "fly" underwater. Many other flightless birds live on islands where there are few predators, so they do not need to fly to escape danger.

At up to 130 lb (60 kg), the southern cassowary is far too heavy to fly.

On the next upstroke, the wing feathers begin to separate again.

On the downstroke, the wing feathers make a smooth, flat surface.

Up and away
The pigeon pulls its wings down. The feathers push against the air, moving the bird up and forward.

! WOW!

Flight muscles may be up to 40 percent of a bird's weight!

Senses

Like us, birds have five senses—sight, hearing, smell, taste, and touch. Some of these are used by certain birds more than others. Most birds have superb eyesight and hearing, and their other senses are poor. However, a few birds depend on smell and taste.

Australian gannet
Front-facing eyes help the gannet track moving fish.

Sight
Birds use sight to get around, find food, stay in touch, and detect enemies. They see in color—often in great detail. Many have eyes that face sideways, but in predatory birds, the eyes usually face forward to target prey.

Eurasian woodcock
Big eyes high up on the head give all-around vision.

Great horned owl
A bowl-shaped face focuses sound toward the owl's hidden ears. The feather tufts are just for show!

Hearing
Birds have excellent hearing. Their ears are inside their heads. The openings lie underneath feathers slightly behind and below each eye. Owls and some other birds can locate prey purely by sound.

Oilbird
To navigate in dark caves, the oilbird makes sounds and then listens for the echoes, like a bat.

Smell

For most birds, smell is not vital. They are attracted by how things look, not by smell or taste. However, vultures can smell the bodies of dead animals from more than 1 mile (1.6 km) away.

Turkey vulture
Huge nostrils help turkey vultures smell their food—dead animals—from far away.

Kiwi
A kiwi has nostrils at the tip of its long bill to sniff out worms.

Bearded barbet
Bristles on this bird's face may help it feel when feeding.

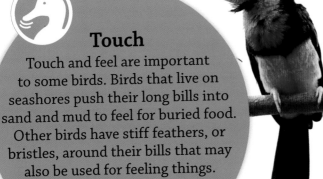

Touch

Touch and feel are important to some birds. Birds that live on seashores push their long bills into sand and mud to feel for buried food. Other birds have stiff feathers, or bristles, around their bills that may also be used for feeling things.

Balancing act

Birds have an excellent sense of balance. Even when asleep, they keep their balance sitting on their perch or standing up.

Sleeping flamingos balance standing on one leg.

Mallard
A mallard's bill is very sensitive. It can feel food in muddy water, where it is difficult to see.

2

Ostrich

1

Osprey

The osprey snatches fish from water.

The ostrich has just two toes on each foot.

A

B

C

Perching feet
In songbirds, all of the toes clamp onto the twig or branch. This stops the birds from falling off.

Gripping feet
The most flexible feet can pick up and hold things. They have two toes at the front and two at the back.

Swimming feet
Some water birds and seabirds have wide webs between their toes to help them paddle and dive.

All about feet

A bird's feet are perfectly suited to its lifestyle. Nearly all birds have four toes, but their feet come in all kinds of shapes, depending on where they live and how they get around and find food. Try this quiz to match each bird with its feet.

Staying warm
Emperor penguins can stand on ice for weeks on end, yet they don't freeze. The blood in their legs is cooled down before it reaches their feet. This stops them from losing valuable body heat through their feet into the ice.

3 Sarus crane

Cranes hunt in wetlands, such as marshes.

4 Mandarin duck

The mandarin duck lives in forest rivers and lakes.

5 Sun parakeet

Parakeets perch with one foot and lift food with the other.

6 Blue tit

Small birds, such as tits, can grip tightly enough to hang upside down.

D

Hunting feet
Birds of prey have powerful feet with sharp claws, called talons, for holding their prey firmly.

E

Wading feet
Long toes keep wading birds from sinking in soft mud and sand.

F

Running feet
Heavy land birds need strong feet and thick, muscular legs for running and walking.

Emperor penguins on Antarctic ice

Blue-footed booby

! **WOW!**

The male blue-footed booby's feet are very attractive to the females.

Bills

At the front of a bird's head is its bill, or beak. It is made of lightweight "jaws" covered in a layer of keratin. Birds depend on their bills for many things. Its size and shape are very good clues to how the bird feeds. Bills can be long or short, straight or curved, and all kinds of different shapes.

! WOW!

Because it gets **worn down**, a bill's keratin covering **never stops** growing.

Slurp

Sword-billed hummingbird

Nectar drinkers

Hummingbirds drink nectar—a sugary fluid made by flowers—by using their long, thin bill like a straw. They push it deep into a flower to reach the nectar.

Stab

Black-crowned night heron

Fish eaters

Herons, storks, and kingfishers have a long, strong, pointed bill shaped like a dagger. This is the perfect shape to catch fish and other prey in water.

American flamingo

Sieve

Soup eaters

Flamingos hold their curved bills upside down in "soupy" water to sift out tiny shrimps and algae.

Golden eagle

Tear

Meat eaters

Carnivorous birds, such as birds of prey, need a powerful, hooked bill. Its tip has a sharp cutting edge for tearing up meat.

Hawfinch

Crack

Seedeaters

Finches have cone-shaped bills that are strong enough to crack open the tough outer cases of seeds.

Red-bellied woodpecker

Drill

Insect eaters

Woodpeckers use their bills to drill holes in tree trunks. Their long tongue then pulls out hidden insect grubs.

Mallard

Skim

Aquatic-life eaters

Ducks and geese have wide, flat bills for skimming food from ponds, lakes, and rivers.

Big boomer

Some birds have extraordinary bills. The male rhinoceros hornbill has a huge, downcurved bill. On top is an extra section that curves upward like a horn. It's used to attract females and works like a loudspeaker, making the bird's booming calls even louder.

Rhinoceros hornbill

Mealtime

Birds are highly active animals, so they need to eat a lot of food. They feed frequently and prefer energy-rich foods. Many birds feed on other animals, and many are omnivores, which means they eat a mixture of animals and plants. Very few birds eat leaves or grass.

Eurasian oystercatcher

Anna's hummingbird

Sipping nectar

Flower nectar is full of sugar. In tropical parts of the world, honeyeaters, sunbirds, and hummingbirds use their long bills and tongues to sip this high-energy fuel.

Mollusk meals

Many shorebirds eat mollusks, such as mussels, clams, and sea snails. Oystercatchers open mollusks by stabbing their hinged shells apart or by hammering them.

Feeding on seeds

Seeds are easily the most popular type of plant food eaten by birds. A huge variety of birds eat them, including sparrows, buntings, and finches. Some birds, such as jays, bury large numbers of seeds to eat later during winter.

Eurasian jay

Blue-footed booby

Violet touraco

Feeding on fruit

In tropical regions, it is usually warm so birds such as touracos can eat fruit all year round. In cooler parts of the world, birds eat fruit mainly in the fall.

Fishy favorites

Some birds locate fish by hovering over water. Others dive in—either from high in the air, such as boobies, or from the surface, such as penguins.

Chestnut-headed bee-eater

American kestrel

Eating insects

Insects are a protein-rich food favored by many birds all over the world. Bee-eaters snatch bees and wasps in midair and bash them to death before eating them!

Meaty meals

Meat-eating birds prey on everything from other birds to mammals, amphibians, reptiles, and fish. Kestrels specialize in hunting large insects and small mammals such as mice.

Let's talk

Birds "talk" in many ways. They may sing, call out, make other noises, or show off dazzling feathers and bold dance moves. Communication is very important in order for birds to stay in touch, defend their territory, attract mates, and warn of danger.

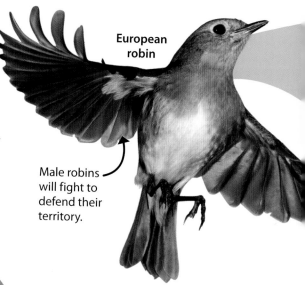

European robin

Male robins will fight to defend their territory.

Nonvocal noises

Some pigeons make sounds by clapping their wings together in flight. Woodpeckers hammer hollow trees to create a drumming noise. Pairs of albatrosses rattle their bills to greet each other.

Dancing birds

Male birds often perform dances to impress females watching them and attract mates. The male ruffed grouse struts around. As he does so, he beats his wings fast and hard to produce a powerful "boom."

Black-browed albatrosses

Black-browed albatrosses pair up for life.

Ruffed grouse

Feathers

Many birds raise their head feathers to show alarm. The color of feathers can send messages, too. When one male European robin sees the red breast of a rival, he will often attack.

This bird copies other animals' alarm calls and then steals their food.

Fork-tailed drongo

Copycats

Parrots, drongos, and mockingbirds are able to mimic sounds they hear. Some of them copy other birds' songs, and some even copy cell phone ring tones!

Songs and calls

Birds sing a wide range of songs. They vary from the bluebird's sweet warbles to trills, chatters, buzzes, croaks, and squeaks. Calls are short, quick sounds that birds use to find each other.

Eastern bluebird

In a Native American myth, the bluebird's song drives away the spirit of winter.

Alarm calls

Chickadees have different alarm calls for different threats. If a predatory bird is flying toward them, they use one call to warn neighbors. However, if the predator is perched, they use another call.

Black-capped chickadee

Male ruffed grouse flap their wings fast to make a booming noise.

Finding a mate

Choosing a partner, or mate, is the most important task a bird faces. Without one, they can't breed and have young. Often the male plays the lead role in forming a couple. To attract a female, he may show off his feathers, dance, or sing. This is called courtship.

Gifts are one way to win over a possible partner. The male hoopoe offers a juicy insect to tempt a female to become his mate.

When the male great frigatebird spots a female, he blows up the stretchy red skin on his throat to make a bright balloon.

Mr. Flamboyant!

Dazzling decor

To impress the females, the male Vogelkop bowerbird makes a tent-like "bower" from sticks. Then he decorates it with flowers, leaves, and berries.

Male and female western grebes dance together to bond. There are several set pieces, including a routine where they rush across the water side by side.

Many male birds, such as this great tit, sing to get females' attention. Each male sings from his own territory, and the ones with the loudest or best voices have the most success.

Pow!

During the breeding season, male ruffs gather at special display arenas. Here, they strut and fight, and visiting females watch the action to decide which males will make the best fathers.

Nests

Most birds make some kind of nest for their eggs and young. A nest stops the eggs from rolling away and breaking, and when the chicks hatch, it helps keep them snug and warm and hides them from enemies. Nests may be very simple, but some are so complex that they take a few weeks to build.

Scrape

Some birds, such as terns, make their nests by scraping out shallow dips in the ground with their feet or bellies. They may then add a lining of grass, feathers, or pebbles.

Arctic tern eggs

Cup-shaped nest

Many birds construct cup-like nests, usually in bushes or trees, or up on ledges. Often they use sticks and twigs, held together with mud, wool, sticky cobwebs, or even spit.

Yellow warbler

PLATFORM

Big birds, such as storks and eagles, need a strong platform to carry their weight. They build the platform from large sticks, and pairs of birds may reuse the same nest over many years.

White storks

Hanging

Weavers and orioles weave dry grass into beautiful hanging nests. Shaped like long socks, they end in chambers for the eggs and young. Safe inside, they cannot be reached by predators.

Entrance at base

Baya weavers

Eastern bluebird

Hole

Holes in trees and walls make cozy nests for birds such as bluebirds, tits, and woodpeckers. They might use existing holes or excavate their own.

SPHERE

Red ovenbird

This unusual type of nest is completely round, like a basketball. Ovenbirds make their spheres out of wet mud, which hardens in the sun, but meadowlarks use grass instead.

Bank swallow

Burrow

Cliffs and sandy banks are perfect nest sites. Many swallows and kingfishers nest here, gradually digging long tunnels, or burrows, for their eggs and young.

Mound

The Australian mallee bird's nest is a giant heap of sand and rotting leaves. The female buries her eggs in the middle of the mound. Heat produced by the rotting leaves keeps the eggs warm.

Mallee bird

91.4°F (33°C)

Pushing away

Next, the chick pushes its head backward and upward as hard as it can. The crack widens.

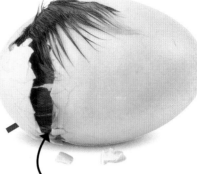

Some of the chick's feathers start to poke through.

Hammering

Between rests, the duckling keeps on hammering at the shell. The chick rotates as it cuts, carving a complete circle in the egg.

Duckling cuts around the entire end of the egg.

Eggs and hatching

A bird's egg is a single, huge cell, with an outer shell for protection. Eggs come in many shapes, sizes, colors, and patterns. Once laid, the eggs are kept warm by the parents, who sit on them until they hatch. Some birds, such as albatrosses, lay a single egg, but partridges can lay 20 or more each year.

Duckling breaks through at the wide end of the egg.

Making a hole

First, the duckling begins chipping away at the inside of the shell. Its bill has a special hard tip for this job, called an "egg tooth."

Don't touch birds' eggs in the wild!

World's smallest egg →

Vervain hummingbird

Cetti's warbler

Cuckoo shrike

American robin

Quail

Ring plover

4

Cracking open
At last, the chick gives one final huge push. The shell cracks into two parts.

What's inside an egg?

The growing chick, or embryo, gets nutrients from the yolk, and water and extra protein from the albumen, or egg white. The shell is breathable—it allows fresh oxygen in and waste carbon dioxide out.

Yolk

Sac full of fluid

Embryo

Albumen

Air space

Chicken embryo

5

Kicking free
By now exhausted, the chick heaves and kicks until it has wriggled out. It has its first taste of freedom in the outside world.

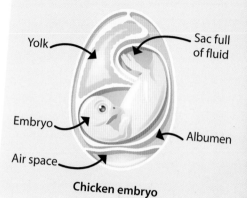

World's biggest egg

6

Free at last!
The duckling rests for a while and lets its feathers dry. Now it's ready to run off and find food, under the watchful eye of its mother.

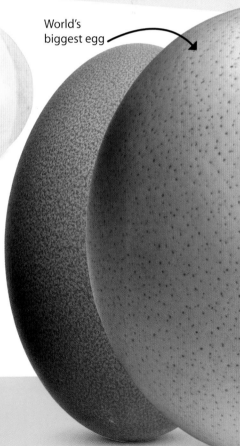

Northern lapwing

Chicken

Osprey

Common guillemot

Southern cassowary

Ostrich

25

Young birds

Some baby birds, such as ducklings, hatch with feathers and can already see and hear. Within a few hours, they are walking around and exploring. However, most birds hatch blind, bald, and weak. They rely on their parents for almost everything.

First days
Black-naped monarchs usually have two or three chicks. They stay in the nest for nearly two weeks. By the end, it is quite a squeeze!

Colorful mouth
The chick's huge orange mouth urges the parent to push food inside.

Open eyes
At first, the chick's eyes stay closed, but after a week they open.

Baby food

The chicks of small birds need feeding every few minutes in the daytime. The chicks of larger birds, such as birds of prey, get fed less often. Parent pigeons and flamingos offer their young a liquid known as "milk," although it is not true milk.

Pigeons feed their chicks "pigeon milk."

The first flight

We take time learning to swim or ride a bicycle, but young birds don't need flying lessons. Flight comes automatically—they do it by instinct. However, at first they are weak and clumsy fliers.

1 Taking off
The parents of a baby chaffinch call to encourage it to fly. Finally, it jumps off the nest and into the air.

The young bird's feathers are not fully grown yet.

2 In the air
Beating its wings a few times, the chaffinch tries to control its descent. Its flight is fluttering and unsteady.

3 Preparing to land
To slow down, the bird holds its wings low and spreads its tail. Its legs act like a brake, and it lands with a sudden bump. Success!

Parenting

Just like human parents, birds work hard to care for their young. Most chicks are helpless—they have to be fed, cleaned, and protected from danger. The parents tuck their offspring into their breast feathers or under their wings to shelter them from bad weather. How long a young bird needs to be looked after varies from about two weeks to several months.

Storing food

Adult pelicans store fish in a massive, stretchy pouch under their bills. When it's full, they fly back to the nest, and the young reach inside for a sloppy meal of half-digested fish paste.

A brown pelican feeding its chicks

Imprinting

Some young birds "imprint" on their mothers. That is, they recognize her and follow her everywhere. This behavior is seen in turkeys, geese, ducks, and some other water birds.

Feeding the young

Parents work nonstop to feed their hungry brood. In many bird species, the nestlings compete for meals, so some may be left out. In others, the parents share the food fairly.

Protection

Baby swans, called cygnets, are able to feed themselves a few hours after hatching. However, they still rely on their parents for protection. Both of the adults guard their brood fiercely.

Trickster birds

The European cuckoo does not raise its young. Instead, it secretly lays its eggs in the nests of other bird species. The eggs look similar, and the other birds are tricked into raising the cuckoo.

Follow the leader
Newly hatched sheldrakes have a powerful urge to imprint on whatever they see first. Usually, this is their mother. In captivity, a bird will occasionally imprint on a person or even an object!

Fast-growing family
A wren-warbler family contains between two and five young. Their busy parents must find enough insects to satisfy their chicks' huge appetites. The parents make thousands of feeding trips during the two to three weeks it takes to raise their young.

Devoted dad
The male mute swan, or cob, is a "stay-at-home dad." Together with the female, or pen, he stays near the cygnets and leads them to safe places to feed. When very young, the cygnets sometimes hitch a ride on his back.

Uninvited guest
A cuckoo chick hatches fast and throws out the other eggs, so it can have all the food to itself. This hedge sparrow does not realize that the enormous youngster is not its own chick!

Living together

Many birds like company, although some live mostly alone or in pairs. Groups of birds are called flocks. Birds form flocks for different reasons. Living together in a flock makes it easier to search for food, spot danger, and chase away predators.

Feeding together
Where there's plenty of food, birds may gather in large numbers. Lakes in Kenya, Africa, attract huge flocks of lesser flamingos to feast on algae and tiny shrimps.

Joining the flock

Birds usually join flocks only at certain times of the day or year. They might gather in the evening to sleep or fly long distances together. Afterward, they go their own separate ways.

A flock of sandhill cranes flies in V formation.

Flying together
Cranes and geese fly in tight V formations. Flying at the front of the flock takes more effort, so they switch positions and take turns being the leader.

! WOW!

Some flamingo flocks contain **hundreds of thousands** of birds!

Parrots such as these galahs roost in flocks.

Resting together
Going to sleep, or roosting, is when birds are most vulnerable. So many species sleep in flocks in safe places, such as tall trees, cliffs, or open water.

Staying healthy

If feathers become dirty or damaged, birds find it difficult to fly and stay warm and dry. So every day, they make sure they clean themselves. Some birds also eat grit, salt, or minerals to help digest their food.

Climb aboard, please!
Wings spread out so ants can reach every feather.

Blue jay letting ants walk over it

Dust bathing
Believe it or not, dust can clean feathers! Birds roll in it and flick it all over their bodies to remove dirt, biting lice, and other pests.

House sparrow enjoying a dust bath

Anting
Some birds encourage ants to crawl on them. The ants release a chemical called formic acid. This might help get rid of pests that harm feathers.

Helping out
A rainbow lorikeet preens the feathers that are difficult to reach on its mate.

Preening
Birds carefully use their bills to preen, or smooth and rearrange their feathers. They pick up a special oil from near their tails and then wipe it across their feathers to waterproof them.

Taking a shower
The freshwater washes
off salt from the sea.

Southern rockhopper penguin bathing
under a waterfall

Sunbathing

Birds like to warm up
in the sunshine. The heat
dries their feathers off. It
also makes it easier for
them to spread their
preening oil.

Drying off
Wet feathers
soon dry
in the
sunshine.

Bathing

Many birds visit pools,
lakes, or rivers to bathe.
On hot days, splashing in
water is also a great way
to cool down.

Wings open
Like a human
sunbather, this
gray heron angles
its body to catch
the sun's rays.

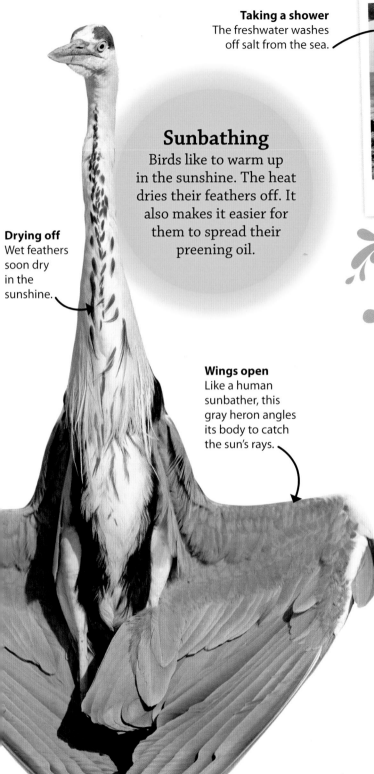

Eating clay

Parrots, such as macaws, often visit
riverbanks to nibble the clay. The salt
and minerals in the clay might protect
them against poisons in the seeds and
unripe fruit they eat.

Red-and-green macaws
gathering on a clay cliff

Survival

Life is full of dangers for birds. Predators—sometimes including other birds—lurk everywhere. Many animals also want to steal their eggs, chicks, or food. Extreme weather can be deadly, too. Fortunately, birds have plenty of survival tactics and tricks to stay safe. If all else fails... they make a quick getaway!

THREAT DISPLAY

GREAT HORNED OWL

A dramatic display is one way to drive off predators. If a great horned owl is approached by a fox or human, it puffs itself up and spreads its wings to appear bigger. The owl also hisses and screams and clacks its bill to sound fearsome.

FIGHT BACK

ARCTIC TERN

When they feel under threat, some birds are ready to attack to protect themselves or their young. Pairs of Arctic terns will dive-bomb any animals that get too close to their nest. Often they draw blood with their sharp, pointed bills.

SMELLY ATTACK

NORTHERN FULMAR CHICK

A fulmar chick is too fat and slow to run away from danger. Instead, it vomits to protect itself from predators such as foxes. The chick opens its bill and squirts a jet of nasty, sticky oil in the face of its enemy. It smells awful!

MOBBING

★ ★

HOUSE CROW

Some birds, such as crows, gang up to drive away a threatening bird of prey. By joining forces, they can all swoop at their target. Eventually, the bird of prey flies off to find somewhere more peaceful. This behavior is called mobbing.

! WOW!

The **common poorwill** is the only bird that **hibernates** to survive winter.

Common poorwill

CAMOUFLAGE

★ ★

GREEN BROADBILL

Many birds have plumage that matches their habitat, so predators don't spot them. This is known as camouflage. The green broadbill is the same shape and color as the leaves in its rain-forest home. When not moving, it blends in perfectly.

PRETENDING

★ ★

KILLDEER

Sometimes birds that nest on the ground play a trick on their enemies. If a predator approaches a killdeer's nest, the parent flutters about as if its wing is broken. The predator thinks the parent would be an easy kill, so it follows it and leaves the nest alone.

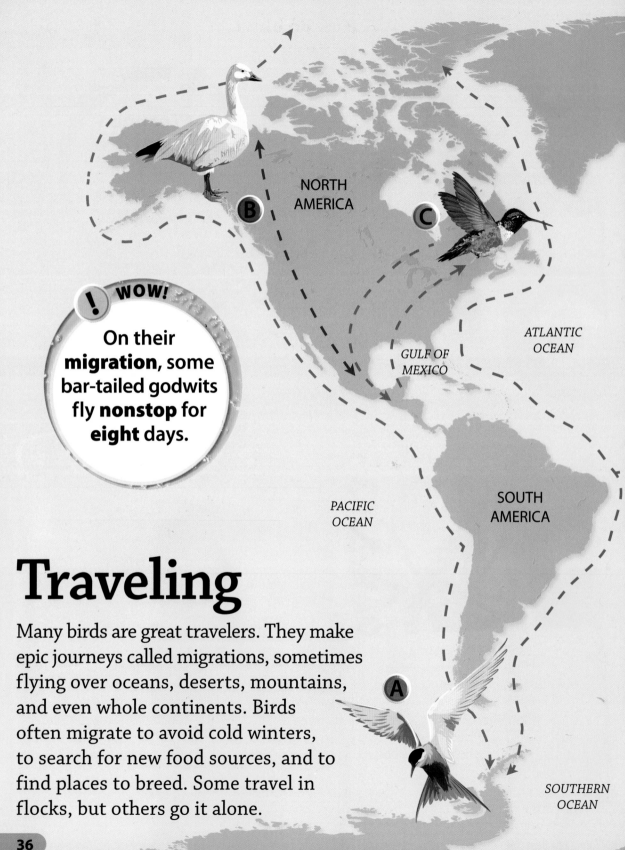

NORTH AMERICA

B

C

ATLANTIC OCEAN

GULF OF MEXICO

! WOW!

On their **migration**, some bar-tailed godwits fly **nonstop** for **eight** days.

PACIFIC OCEAN

SOUTH AMERICA

Traveling

Many birds are great travelers. They make epic journeys called migrations, sometimes flying over oceans, deserts, mountains, and even whole continents. Birds often migrate to avoid cold winters, to search for new food sources, and to find places to breed. Some travel in flocks, but others go it alone.

A

SOUTHERN OCEAN

ARCTIC
OCEAN

How do birds navigate?

Birds check the position of the sun and stars to find their way. They also have an internal "compass," which senses the earth's magnetic field. By day, they look out for familiar landmarks on the ground below, too.

Migrating snow geese

EUROPE

ASIA

MEDITERRANEAN
SEA

 E

 D

AFRICA

INDIAN
OCEAN

OCEANIA

Key to routes

 A Arctic tern
This seabird's trip, from the Arctic to the Antarctic and back again, can be about 43,500 miles (70,000 km)!

 B Snow goose
In the fall, snow geese fly from Canada to spend winter in the United States and Mexico. They head north again in the spring.

 C Ruby-throated hummingbird
This tiny bird is able to fly nonstop across the Gulf of Mexico.

 D European white stork
Storks avoid long, tiring sea crossings. They take the shortest routes across the Mediterranean Sea when they migrate.

 E Demoiselle crane
Cranes that nest in Mongolia and China spend winter in India. To get there, they must fly over the mighty Himalayas mountain range.

Birds of prey

Birds of prey are expert hunters. They use speed or surprise to catch their food and attack with deadly claws. Some birds of prey snatch fish from water; some hit birds in midair; and others lift animals off the ground. They tear up the meal with their sharp, hooked bills. Birds of prey are also called raptors.

Hawk

Hawks are fierce hunters with broad wings and strong claws. They live in many habitats, including grasslands and forests. They usually feed on small mammals, reptiles, and birds.

Red-tailed hawk

Osprey

The osprey has such sharp eyesight that it can spot fish swimming underwater. It dives to seize the fish, and sharp spines on its claws help grip the slippery prey.

Eagle

Eagles are large and powerful enough to catch prey as big as deer or monkeys. They spot their meals while soaring high up in the sky and then swoop down for the kill.

Bald eagle

Falcon

Falcons are the fastest-flying birds of prey. They eat small birds and mammals, reptiles, and insects. They snatch prey with their strong claws but kill it with their sharp bills.

Lanner falcon

Secretary bird

The secretary bird attacks from the ground rather than the air. It uses its long, powerful legs to stun a snake by stomping on it. The bird then kills the prey by stabbing it with its back claw.

Vulture

Vultures are the largest meat-eating birds. They soar high in the sky on huge wings, searching for food. They feast on the remains of dead animals. By clearing away the bodies, they stop disease from spreading.

Rüppell's vulture

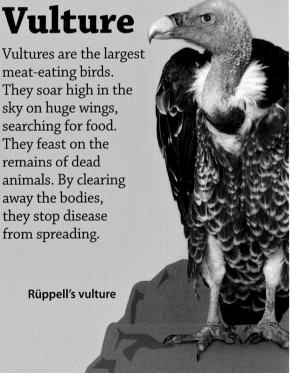

Interview with...

We talked to Dr. Andrew Digby, a scientist who lives in New Zealand and studies kākāpō (kah-kuh-POH) and takahē (tah-KAH-hey). These are two very rare, protected species of bird that are found only in New Zealand.

Q: We know it has something to do with birds, but what is your actual job?

A: I'm the scientist for the kākāpō and takahē conservation programs in New Zealand. These are two big, flightless birds. The kākāpō is a nocturnal parrot, and the takahē is a member of the rail family, which also includes moorhens and swamphens. My job is to do research to help us better protect them.

Q: What made you decide to work in bird conservation?

A: Birds are amazing! I've been fascinated by them since I was very young, growing up in Britain. New Zealand has some very special and rare birds, and they need urgent help.

Q: Why are kākāpō and takahē so rare?

Both were once common in New Zealand. When human settlers arrived, they brought dogs, cats, and stoats with them. Unable to defend themselves well against these new predators, kākāpō and takahē gradually disappeared until they became almost extinct. Also, much of the forest and scrubland where they lived was cleared to make farmland.

Q: What is a usual workday for you?

A: There's no such thing, and that makes this job so special. Some days, I might be analyzing data on a computer or talking at a conference. On other days, I might be in a helicopter in the mountains tracking takahē or climbing a tree to catch a kākāpō on a beautiful remote island.

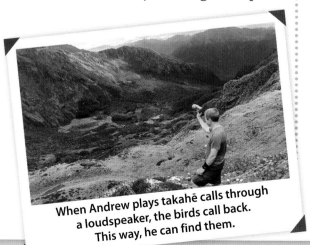

When Andrew plays takahē calls through a loudspeaker, the birds call back. This way, he can find them.

This recently hatched kākāpō chick is being fed by syringe.

A takahē peeps out of the undergrowth.

This kākāpō is called Mahli. Like all other kākāpō, she lives on a predator-free island.

Q: Do you use any special equipment?

We have lots of special technology to help us look after the birds. Every kākāpō wears a transmitter to enable us to find it. These also record their activity, so we can tell—from anywhere in the world—when they've mated or are sick.

Q: What's the best thing about your job?

A: Being able to work with these incredible birds in some amazing places. Also seeing the amazement on a person's face when they meet a kākāpō for the first time! They're always surprised how big they are.

Q: What's the most difficult thing about your job?

A: When a kākāpō or takahē dies. There are so few left—about 150 kākāpō and 350 takahē. Each death is a blow.

Q: What are the biggest threats facing these birds today, and how do you help them?

A: Kākāpō are threatened by disease and infertility, which means they have problems having young. Only about half of their eggs hatch. We work hard to ensure that every chick that hatches survives, and we monitor them for ill health. All kākāpō now live on predator-free islands. Some takahē also live on such islands, but the ones that do not are threatened by stoats. We trap these predators where takahē live.

Q: Do you have a favorite bird?

A: Sinbad the kākāpō is my favorite. He's very special because he's genetically different from, or not closely related to, most of the other kākāpō. So we really need him to become a father. He's also very friendly!

Sinbad hatched in 1998. Kākāpō can live for as long as 90 years.

Birds under threat

More and more birds are under threat. The total number of bird species at risk is about 1,500 worldwide. When a species is threatened, it means it might become extinct, or disappear forever. The main causes of extinction are humans destroying habitats, hunting, pollution, and earth's changing climate.

Great hornbill

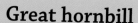

Cutting down forests for wood or to create fields and towns is a serious threat. This is called deforestation. Large areas of the great hornbill's tropical forest habitat in India have been lost.

Flesh-footed shearwater

Humans are catching more and more fish and not leaving enough for seabirds, such as the flesh-footed shearwater, to eat. Seabirds are also at risk from plastic pollution. About 90 percent of the world's seabirds have plastic in their stomachs.

Condor rescue

The mighty California condor is the largest bird in North America. In the 20th century, the species nearly died out. Many condors were killed by hunters or died after being poisoned. In 1987, just 27 were left, so a rescue plan was launched, and the condors were taken into captivity for breeding. Since 1992, conservationists—people who protect wildlife—have been releasing some of the birds back into the wild. There are now more than 460 condors.

Conservationists saved California condors from extinction.

Turtledove

Modern farming often uses chemical fertilizers and pesticides. Fields then have fewer wild flower seeds and insects, which are the main food of farmland birds such as Europe's turtledove. Farmers also remove hedges and trees, leaving fewer places for birds to rest and nest.

I'iwi

Birds that live on islands have only small populations, so they can quickly get into trouble. The i'iwi—you say its name "ee-ee-vee"—is found in Hawaii. It is now uncommon, because its forest home has been cleared, and it catches a disease spread by mosquitoes.

Seabirds

Oceans and seas cover 70 percent of the earth's surface, and birds found here are great travelers. Some soar over the waves, diving or swooping for food, while others swim. All seabirds must return to land to breed.

Atlantic puffin

Small and plump, the puffin looks like a penguin, but it can fly as well as swim and dive. It is nicknamed "the parrot of the sea" due to its colorful bill.

FACT FILE

» **Location:** North Atlantic Ocean. It nests in burrows on cliff tops.

» **Food:** Small fish. It can carry 10–20 of them in its beak at a time!

» **Fun fact:** The bright outer part of the puffin's bill falls off in winter.

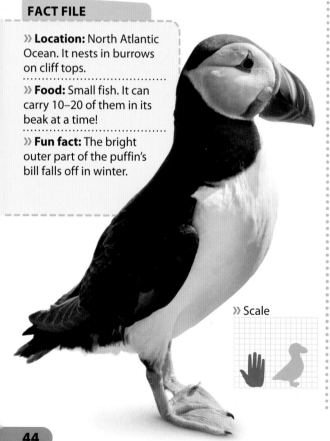

» Scale

The albatross's wingspan stretches up to 11 1/2 ft (3.5 m).

! WOW!

The **wandering albatross** is the **largest** flying bird in the **world.**

Wilson's petrel

Only as big as a sparrow, this tiny but tough seabird is one of the world's most common birds. There are tens of millions of Wilson's petrels out at sea.

» Scale

FACT FILE

» **Location:** Atlantic Ocean and oceans across the southern half of the world

» **Food:** Krill, which are small, shrimp-like animals, and small fish

» **Fun fact:** This bird flies so close to the sea that it seems to be walking on water.

Wandering albatross

Huge wings let the albatross soar over stormy seas for hours on end. It flies vast distances in search of food, which it finds by smell. Albatrosses nest in colonies on remote islands.

» Scale

FACT FILE

» **Location:** Southern oceans

» **Food:** Squid, fish, and jellyfish

» **Fun fact:** Albatrosses can live for 60 years, and they keep the same partners for life.

Great frigatebird

A superb and elegant flier, the frigatebird is a thief. It chases other seabirds to steal their fish, so it's sometimes known as the "pirate bird."

FACT FILE

» **Location:** Tropical parts of the Pacific and Indian Oceans

» **Food:** Fish stolen from other birds

» **Fun fact:** Unlike most seabirds, frigatebirds do not have waterproof plumage, so they never land on water.

» Scale

Northern gannet

This magnificent seabird dives like a bullet to catch fish. Air sacs on its throat and neck protect the bird when it hits the water, like the airbags in a car.

» Scale

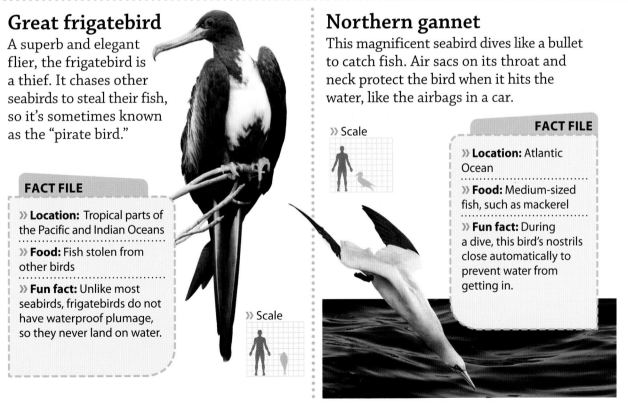

FACT FILE

» **Location:** Atlantic Ocean

» **Food:** Medium-sized fish, such as mackerel

» **Fun fact:** During a dive, this bird's nostrils close automatically to prevent water from getting in.

Shorebirds

Shores, or coasts, are a food-rich habitat for birds. Daily tides wash a huge variety of small animal prey onto sandy and rocky beaches. Muddy shores are full of buried shellfish and worms.

! WOW!

Female raptors, or birds of prey, are always **bigger** than the males.

White-tailed sea eagle

This impressive, powerful raptor snatches fish from the sea's surface. Seabirds as large as ducks are also on its menu. Pairs nest on sea cliffs.

» Scale

FACT FILE

» **Location:** Northern Europe and Asia

» **Food:** Mainly fish, but also birds and carrion (flesh of dead animals)

» **Fun fact:** Legends say this eagle can carry away small children. They're not true, of course!

Powerful hold
Sharp talons firmly grip a wriggling fish.

FACT FILE

» **Location:** Coasts worldwide

» **Food:** Small invertebrates, such as sand crabs

» **Fun fact:** The sanderling flies off to breed in the high Arctic, where there is daylight 24 hours each day in the summer.

FACT FILE

» **Location:** North and South America

» **Food:** Fish, frogs, crabs, and other aquatic animals

» **Fun fact:** In summer, skin on the snowy egret's face changes from yellow to red.

Sanderling

This highly active wading bird runs up and down in the surf on sandy beaches. It rushes out to snatch prey and then darts back before the next wave breaks.

Snowy egret

This egret lives on all kinds of coasts and wetlands. During the breeding season, it nests in large colonies in treetops.

» Scale

Plumage changes color in the breeding season.

» Scale

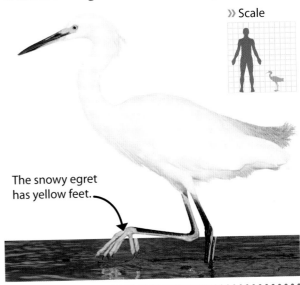

The snowy egret has yellow feet.

Great black-backed gull

The world's largest gull has a massive bill. Like many gulls, it will eat almost anything. Young birds are brown and take four years to become black-and-white adults.

This bird is strong enough to catch puffins and swallow them whole.

» Scale

FACT FILE

» **Location:** North Atlantic Ocean and northern Europe

» **Food:** Fish, seabird chicks, and animals up to the size of rabbits

» **Fun fact:** This gull loves to visit garbage dumps for scraps.

Wetland birds

Ponds, lakes, streams, rivers, and marshes are great habitats for birds. Many species that live here wade through the shallows and waterside plants. Others dive or swim to find food. If the water freezes in winter, the birds will travel to find clear water.

Eurasian kingfisher

Waiting on a branch, the kingfisher scans the water below for movement. Then it suddenly dives to catch its prey. It digs a nesting burrow in sandy riverbanks.

» Scale

Quick dive
A kingfisher dives up to 3 ft (1 m) deep. The bird remains underwater for just a second.

African jacana

The jacana lives in marshes and swamps. It has enormously long toes that spread out its weight. This lets the bird walk across water lilies and other floating plants without sinking.

FACT FILE

» **Location:** Tropical and southern Africa

» **Food:** Insects, worms, snails, and other small water animals

» **Fun fact:** The male jacana tucks his chicks under his wings to carry them.

Ruddy sheldrake

Lakes and rivers are the home of this large duck. It feeds on grassy banks and in shallow water, mostly at night. After breeding, the adults regrow their wing feathers and can't fly for a month.

» Scale

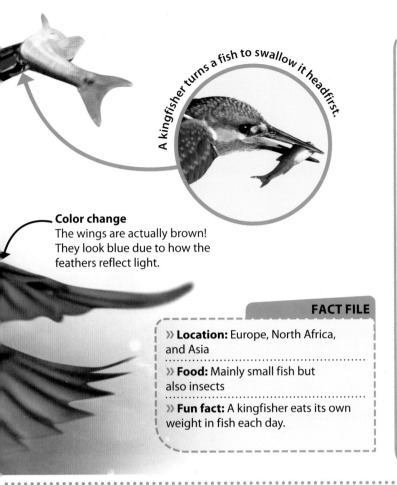

A kingfisher turns a fish to swallow it headfirst.

Color change
The wings are actually brown! They look blue due to how the feathers reflect light.

FACT FILE

» **Location:** Europe, North Africa, and Asia

» **Food:** Mainly small fish but also insects

» **Fun fact:** A kingfisher eats its own weight in fish each day.

How did spoonbills get their name?

Spoonbills are heron-like birds, and they own one of the strangest bills in the world. It is long, flat, and rounded at the end—just like a huge spoon. The bird sweeps it half-open through water to feel for prey.

A European spoonbill eats a fish.

FACT FILE

» **Location:** Central and southern Asia

» **Food:** Leaves, seeds, and insects

» **Fun fact:** People of the Buddhist religion regard this duck as sacred, so they protect it.

Sora

With its thin body, the sora can squeeze through gaps in reeds and other marsh plants. This shy bird is more often heard than seen.

FACT FILE

» **Location:** North and South America

» **Food:** Leaves, seeds, and insects

» **Fun fact:** The sora makes a strange "whee-hee-hee" call.

» Scale

» Scale

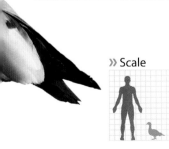
» Scale

Woodland birds

Woods and forests provide birds with plenty of places to feed, hide, and nest. In northern and southern parts of the world, there is the most food in spring and summer, when insects are active. In the tropics, however, woodlands offer lots of food all year round.

FACT FILE

» **Location:** China

» **Food:** Seeds, berries, and insects

» **Fun fact:** Female pheasants are dull brown, which keeps them hidden when sitting on their nests.

Golden pheasant

This spectacular bird lives in shady woodlands in China's mountains. It usually walks quietly among the trees, but it can fly to escape danger.

The male's tail feathers are much longer than his body.

Green woodpecker

Not all woodpeckers hammer on trees. This one prefers to feed on the ground, where it hunts ants. Its long, super-sticky tongue licks them out of their nests.

» Scale

» Scale

FACT FILE

» **Location:** Europe

» **Food:** Mostly ants

» **Fun fact:** The green woodpecker's call sounds a little like human laughter.

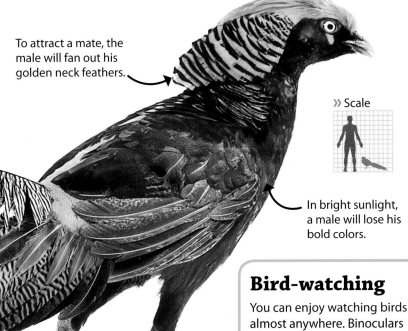

To attract a mate, the male will fan out his golden neck feathers.

» Scale

In bright sunlight, a male will lose his bold colors.

! WOW!

In China, **pheasants** are a sign of **good luck** and **great beauty**!

Bird-watching

You can enjoy watching birds almost anywhere. Binoculars will give you a closer view, but they're not essential. The golden rule of bird-watching is to be quiet and keep your eyes and ears open.

Lilac-breasted roller

To get a good view, this bird perches on a high branch. It then swoops fast and acrobatically to snatch prey on the ground below.

FACT FILE

» **Location:** Tropical Africa

» **Food:** Large insects and lizards

» **Fun fact:** The lilac-breasted roller is the national bird of Kenya, Africa.

» Scale

FACT FILE

» **Location:** United States and Canada

» **Food:** Seeds, berries, leaves, and insects

» **Fun fact:** Males have a wobbly flap of red skin under their chins, called a wattle.

Wild turkey

This huge, heavy bird struts through the woods of North America. All types of domestic turkey are descended from it.

Rain-forest birds

More birds are found in tropical rain forests than anywhere else. Here it is warm and sunny all year round. Rain-forest birds often eat fruit or insects, and they frequently gather in flocks. We are cutting the world's rain forests down at a rapid rate, and this is putting many species in danger.

! WOW!

Aztec people believed that **toucan bills** were made from **rainbows.**

Back rest
When asleep, the toucan rests its bill along its back.

Harpy eagle

This huge eagle builds its nest in the emergent layer. It patrols the canopy to hunt for mammals, snatching prey with its giant feet and talons.

» Scale

FACT FILE

» **Location:** Central and South America

» **Food:** Sloths, monkeys, and other rain-forest mammals

» **Fun fact:** At 5 in (13 cm) long, this bird's talons are longer than the claws of a grizzly bear!

African dwarf kingfisher

This tiny bird has jewel-like feathers, but it is very hard to spot as it perches in dark corners of the understory. Unlike other kingfishers, it often lives far from water.

Toco toucan

It may look clumsy, but the toucan's bill is ideal for picking fruit from the tips of branches in the forest canopy. The edges are sharp and cut like a knife.

Hollow inside
The giant bill is light, because it has thin sides and hollow bone.

» Scale

FACT FILE

» **Location:** South America

» **Food:** Mainly fruit

» **Fun fact:** Toucans prefer to hop from branch to branch, rather than fly.

Rain-forest layers

Rain-forest trees can be giants. Each forest level, from sunny treetops to the dark forest floor, is home to different types of birds.

Emergent layer

Canopy

Understory

Forest floor

» Scale

» Scale

FACT FILE

» **Location:** Tropical Africa

» **Food:** Large insects, spiders, lizards, and frogs

» **Fun fact:** At just 4 in (10 cm) long, this is the world's smallest kingfisher.

Red jungle fowl

If you think this bird looks like a rooster, you would be right. This forest-floor species is the ancestor of all the 20 billion domestic chickens alive today.

FACT FILE

» **Location:** Southeast Asia

» **Food:** Seeds, berries, insects, and other small animals

» **Fun fact:** The jungle fowl was first kept as a domestic bird at least 5,000 years ago.

Desert birds

Hot, sandy, and very dry... deserts are tough places to live. However, even here, there are birds to be found. Their main challenges are how to find drinking water and shelter from the baking sunshine. Food can also be scarce, and birds may have to search far and wide for it.

» Scale

Lappet-faced vulture

This huge vulture bullies smaller vultures so it gets to feed first at carcasses. Its massive bill rips open thick skin and crunches bone.

White "eyebrows" give a fierce expression.

Elf owl

By day, the elf owl often hides in holes inside tall, desert cacti. At nightfall, it comes out to hunt insects by pouncing on them.

» Scale

FACT FILE

» **Location:** Southern United States and Mexico

» **Food:** Mainly moths, beetles, and other insects

» **Fun fact:** This tiny, sparrow-sized bird is the smallest owl on earth.

Greater roadrunner

With its strong legs, the roadrunner sprints over bare stony ground at up to 18 mph (30 kph). In the air, though, it is less spectacular and flies weakly.

Its long tail is held out behind for balance.

FACT FILE

» **Location:** Africa

» **Food:** Carcasses (bodies of dead animals)

» **Fun fact:** This bird has a bare head and neck—if these areas had feathers, they would get soaked in blood when the bird ate.

» Scale

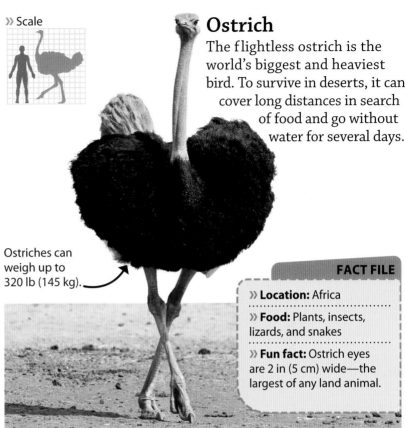

Ostrich

The flightless ostrich is the world's biggest and heaviest bird. To survive in deserts, it can cover long distances in search of food and go without water for several days.

Ostriches can weigh up to 320 lb (145 kg).

FACT FILE

» **Location:** Africa

» **Food:** Plants, insects, lizards, and snakes

» **Fun fact:** Ostrich eyes are 2 in (5 cm) wide—the largest of any land animal.

---

has a strong bill or bashing prey against rocks.

» Scale

FACT FILE

» **Location:** Southern United States and Mexico

» **Food:** Scorpions, spiders, insects, lizards, and snakes

» **Fun fact:** A roadrunner seizes a scorpion's tail before it can get stung.

» Scale

Spotty, sand-colored feathers provide camouflage.

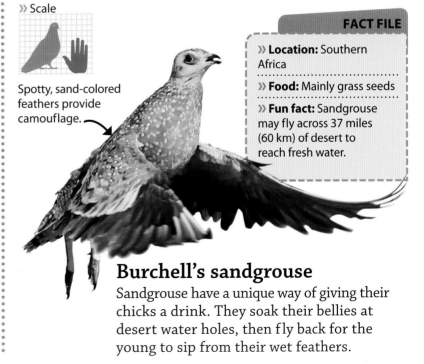

FACT FILE

» **Location:** Southern Africa

» **Food:** Mainly grass seeds

» **Fun fact:** Sandgrouse may fly across 37 miles (60 km) of desert to reach fresh water.

Burchell's sandgrouse

Sandgrouse have a unique way of giving their chicks a drink. They soak their bellies at desert water holes, then fly back for the young to sip from their wet feathers.

Polar birds

The Arctic and Antarctic are extremely cold but full of food for birds. Even better, it is light 24 hours a day in summer, so they can feed around the clock. Huge numbers of seabirds and shorebirds visit to raise their young. Most leave before the fierce, dark polar winter returns.

! WOW!

Emperor penguins can **dive to depths** of **1,600 ft** (500 m).

Emperor penguin

Protected by its thick fat, this penguin is one of the few birds to stay in Antarctica during winter. Like all birds, it is warm-blooded. Groups must huddle together to preserve precious body heat.

» Scale

FACT FILE

» **Location:** Antarctica

» **Food:** Fish and krill (shrimp-like animals)

» **Fun fact:** Emperor penguins keep their single eggs on top of their feet to keep them off the freezing ice.

Long-tailed jaeger

In summer, the long-tailed jaeger heads north to the Arctic. Small rodents called lemmings are its favorite prey. In winter, it flies south and hunts fish instead.

Long, pointed wings allow for superb acrobatic flying.

» Scale

FACT FILE

» **Location:** The Arctic in summer and southern oceans in winter

» **Food:** Lemmings and fish

» **Fun fact:** When lemmings are scarce, the jaeger chooses not to have young that year.

Middle two tail feathers are much longer.

FACT FILE

» **Location:** Arctic seas

» **Food:** Small crustaceans and fish

» **Fun fact:** When full-grown, little auk chicks leap from their cliff ledge into the sea far below.

» Scale

FACT FILE

» **Location:** Arctic seas

» **Food:** Clams, mussels, and other mollusks

» **Fun fact:** Female eiders pluck soft feathers from their breasts to make cozy nests.

Little auk

This little seabird is a relative of the puffin. It nests on sea cliffs in the Arctic in enormous colonies. Some colonies have millions of birds!

To attract mates, male eiders have brighter colors in the breeding season.

King eider

These tough ducks swim and dive in freezing, stormy Arctic seas. Flocks of them often gather on floating sea ice to rest.

Small wings act like flippers underwater.

» Scale

Bird facts and figures

Birds are amazing animals. Here are some weird and wonderful facts that you can impress your friends with!

The song of the **EUROPEAN WREN** has more than **700** notes per minute.

Male

Female

People once thought that **male and female ECLECTUS PARROTS** were **different species** because they look so **different**.

EURASIAN MAGPIES are one of only a few animals, other than humans, that are able to **recognize themselve** in a **mirror**.

1,000,000

The biggest flocks of red-billed queleas contain more than one million birds.

3,730

A wandering albatross was recorded traveling 3,730 miles (6,000 km) in 12 days.

The **SOOTY TERN** *SLEEPS* during flight. Only **half of its brain** dozes at a time.

Hummingbirds are the only birds that can fly backward.

Legs have strong, solid bones.

The **bee hummingbird** of Cuba is the **world's smallest** bird. At about $2^{1}/_{5}$ **in** (5.5 cm) long, it can perch on the top of a pencil.

An **ostrich** can run **43 mph** (70 kph) **at full speed.** That's **as fast as a racehorse**!

2,000

A green woodpecker eats as many as 2,000 ants in a day.

160

There may be as many as 160 eyespots on the tail of an Indian peacock.

Glossary

Here are the meanings of some words that are useful for you to know when learning all about birds.

ancestor Animal to which a more recent animal is related

binoculars Instrument, made up of two small telescopes, used to view things that are far away

bond Form a close relationship

bower Shady place under the leaves and branches of a tree

Blue-footed booby

breeding season Time of the year when animals come together to mate

brood Group of young birds from the same nest

burrow Tunnel or hole dug by a bird or other animal to live in

captivity State of not living in the wild. Zoo animals live in captivity

carbon dioxide Waste gas produced by the body of an animal

cell Part of the body with a specific job. Most cells are very tiny, but the inside of an egg is one huge cell

climate Weather patterns for a particular area

colony Large group of birds living in one place to breed or roost

compass Instrument used to find directions

courtship Types of animal behavior that are aimed at attracting a mate

crest Upright feathers on the top of a bird's head

crustaceans Group of invertebrates that includes crabs, lobsters, and shrimp

deforestation Destruction of forests

digest Break down food inside the body into substances that the body can use

domestic Word used to describe animals kept on farms or as pets

earth's magnetic field Force field surrounding the earth

embryo Unborn or unhatched baby

evolve Change, over many generations, to form new species

extinct Died out. An extinct species no longer has any living members

fertilizer Chemical or a natural substance put on soil to help plants grow

gravity Force that pulls objects toward the ground

habitat Place where a bird lives, such as a woodland or wetland

hibernate Enter a deep sleep-like state during winter

instinct Natural reaction performed without having to learn it

invertebrate Type of animal with no backbone, such as an insect or mollusk

lice Tiny wingless insects that live on the skin of other animals; singular is louse

lift Force needed to lift an object

mineral Natural substance in rocks or the ground

mollusks Large group of invertebrates, including snails, mussels, clams, squid, and octopuses

navigate Find the right direction in which to travel

nutrients Types of food that living things need to survive

omnivore Animal that eats both plants and other animals

oxygen Gas that most living things need to survive

perching Alighting or resting on something, such as a twig or branch, and using the feet to grip

pesticide Chemical that farmers use to control pests, such as insects and weeds

plumage All the feathers on a bird

polar Word used to describe areas near the North or South Pole

pollution Waste that has been dumped in water, in the air, or on land

predator Animal that lives by hunting and eating other animals

soar Fly without flapping the wings

species Specific types of animals or plants with shared features that can mate and produce young together

Wild turkey

territory Area held by an animal. Birds often defend their territory from intruders

transmitter Electronic device that sends out signals

tropical Area or a climate with hot temperatures and high rainfall

vertebrate Animal that has a backbone, or spine

warm-blooded Able to keep a constant body temperature. Birds and mammals are warm-blooded

yolk Yellow part inside a bird's egg. It contains fat and protein to feed the developing chick

Index

Acknowledgments

The publisher would like to thank the following people for their assistance in the preparation of this book: Seeta Parmar and Jack Shelton for editorial assistance; Roohi Rais for design assistance; Polly Goodman for proofreading; Helen Peters for compiling the index; Dan Crisp and Mohd Zishan for illustrations; and Dr. Andrew Digby for his "Interview with..." interview.

The publisher would like to thank the following for their kind permission to reproduce their photographs:

(Key: a-above; b-below/bottom; c-center; f-far; l-left; r-right; t-top)

1 iStockphoto.com: BirdHunter591. **2 Dreamstime.com:** PeterWaters (br). **3 123RF.com:** Magdalena Ruseva (bl). **Dreamstime.com:** Shawn Hempel (br); Ondřej Prosický (clb); **Getty Images:** Joel Sartore, National Geographic Photo Ark (bc); UniversalImagesGroup (tr). **4 Dreamstime.com:** Dndavis (crb); Brian Kushner (c); Troy Lilly / Forestphotoart (cb). **4–5 Dreamstime.com:** Nejron (t). **5 Dreamstime.com:** Dndavis (bl). **Getty Images:** Piero M. Bianchi (crb). **6–7 123RF.com:** szefei (Background). **Getty Images:** Martin Harvey. **7 123RF.com:** Ross Taylor (bc). **Alamy Stock Photo:** Avalon / Photoshot License (cra); Gabbro (crb). **Dorling Kindersley:** Natural History Museum, London (bl). **Science Photo Library:** Dennis Kunkel Microscopy (cb). **9 Alamy Stock Photo:** imageBROKER (cra). **10 Alamy Stock Photo:** imageBROKER (tr). **Dreamstime.com:** Martin Grossman (br); Viter8 (cr). **11 123RF.com:** Eric Isselee / isselee (cla). **Dreamstime.com:** Dejavu Designs (cb); Feng Yu (bl); Yaroslava Polosina (tr). **Getty Images:** Frank Krahmer (crb). **12 Getty Images:** Vicki Jauron, Babylon and Beyond Photography (t). **13 123RF.com:** Magdalena Ruseva (ca). **Depositphotos Inc:** MennoSchaefer (tr). **Dreamstime.com:** Evgenia Bolyukh (ca/Parrot); Martinmark (bc). **iStockphoto.com:** Sabirmallick (tl). **Courtesy of the National Science Foundation:** Greg Neri (bl). **14 123RF.com:** Marat Roytman (clb). **Dreamstime.com:** Ondřej Prosický (cl); Edwin Verin (r). **15 123RF.com:** Mr.Narin Sapaisarn (br). **Depositphotos Inc:** Mayerberg (tl); mcseem (c). **Dreamstime.com:** Eng101 (tr); Rebecca Warren (cl). **16 Dreamstime.com:** Steve Byland (cl). **iStockphoto.com:** Volodymyr Kucherenko (br). **SuperStock:** Rob Kuiper / Minden Pictures (cr). **17 Dreamstime.com:** Gualberto Becerra (clb); Burt Johnson (tl); David Carillet (tr); Mr.jarun Sangkhrim (cb); **iStockphoto.com:** mzphoto (b). **Getty Images:** Rolf Muller (tr). **18–19 Alamy Stock Photo:** Don Johnston (b). **19 Alamy Stock Photo:** Jelldragon (tr). **Dreamstime.com:** Brian Lasenby (br). **Getty Images:** Joel Sartore, National Geographic Photo Ark (c). **20 Alamy Stock Photo:** Nature Picture Library (b). **Dreamstime.com:** Donyanedomam (cr). **naturepl.com:** Bence Mate (cl). **21 Alamy Stock Photo:** Ondrej Pelanek (b). **Dreamstime.com:** Geza Farkas (cl). **Getty Images:** Reed Kaestner (tr). **22 Dreamstime.com:** Kyslynskyy (br); Terence Smith (cra). **iStockphoto.com:** Dantesattic (cl). **23 Alamy Stock Photo:** Danita Delimont (c). **Dreamstime.com:** Jevtic (cr); Korakot Khayankarnnavee (tl). **iStockphoto.com:** SteveByland (tr). **Rex by Shutterstock:** Auscape / UIG (b). **24 Dorling Kindersley:** Natural History Museum, London (bc, bc/Cuckoo Shrike egg, br, br/Common Quail egg, fbr). **25 Alamy Stock Photo:** BIOSPHOTO (br). **Dorling Kindersley:** Natural History Museum, London (fbl, bc, bc/Common Guillemot egg). **26–27 123RF.com:** kajornyot. **27 Dreamstime.com:** Khunaspix (tc). **28 FLPA:** Tui De Roy / Minden Pictures (bl). **28–29 Alamy Stock Photo:** Paul Miguel (cb); Southmind (t). **FLPA:** Neil Bowman (bc). **iStockphoto.com:** Rohani_tanasal (ca). **30–31 iStockphoto.com:** Ivanmateev. **31 Alamy Stock Photo:** Design Pics Inc (cra); Russotwins (cl). **32 Dreamstime.com:** Dmitry Maslov (c); PeterWaters (bl). **ME Raine:** (cra). **33 Alamy Stock Photo:** blickwinkel (l). **Dreamstime.com:** Dalia Kvedaraite (tr). **iStockphoto.com:** wilsondmir (br). **34 Alamy Stock Photo:** imageBROKER (clb). **naturepl.com:** Andy Trowbridge (crb). **35 Alamy Stock Photo:** FLPA (clb); James Schaedig (crb). **Depositphotos Inc:** Utopia_88 (tl, ftl). **Dreamstime.com:** Pnwnature (cr). **37 Dreamstime.com:** Derrick Neill (tr). **38 Getty Images:** Garry Ridsdale (b). **iStockphoto.com:** ElementalImaging (cr). **39 Dreamstime.com:** Jahoo (t/Background). **Getty Images:** Roger de la Harpe / UIG (cl); UniversalImagesGroup (t). **40 Andrew Digby:** (br). **Daryl Eason:** (bl). **Deidre Vercoe:** (tl). **41 Matu Booth:** (bc). **Andrew Digby:** (tl, tr). **42 Alamy Stock Photo:** David Tipling Photo Library (br). **iStockphoto.com:** Casper1774Studio (bl). **43 Dreamstime.com:** Rudmer Zwerver (bl). **iStockphoto.com:** JohnMernick (br). **naturepl.com:** John Cancalosi (tr). **44–45 Alamy Stock Photo:** Roland Knauer (t). **44 Alamy Stock Photo:** robertharding (crb). **Fotolia:** Stefan Zeitz / Lux (bl). **45 Alamy Stock Photo:** Avico Ltd (br); National Geographic Image Collection (cb). **46 Depositphotos Inc:** Giedriius. **47 123RF.com:** Abi Warner (cl). **Alamy Stock Photo:** Martin Fowler (bl). **Dreamstime.com:** Mike Jackson (cr). **48 Dreamstime.com:** Tobie1953 (bl). **iStockphoto.com:** DaddyBit (br). **48–49 iStockphoto.com:** MikeLane45 (t). **49 Alamy Stock Photo:** Nature Picture Library (cr). **Dreamstime.com:** Howardk3 (tc); Glenn Price (bc). **50–51 Depositphotos Inc:** mauro.grigollo (t). **50 123RF.com:** Berangere Duforets (br). **Dreamstime.com:** Ondřej Prosický (bl). **51 Dreamstime.com:** Bruce Macqueen (b). **52 Getty Images:** Barry B. Doyle (bl); Carlton Ward (br). **52–53 Dreamstime.com:** Andrew Allport (t). **54 Alamy Stock Photo:** Anthony Mercieca / Dembinsky Photo Associates (bl). **54–55 Alamy Stock Photo:** National Geographic Image Collection (t). **iStockphoto.com:** Twildlife (b). **55 Dreamstime.com:** Ecophoto (crb); Mikelane45 (tr). **56 123RF.com:** Raldi Somers / gentoomultimedia. **57 Alamy Stock Photo:** André Gilden (br). **Dreamstime.com:** Erectus (bl). **Getty Images:** Dieter Hopf (tr). **58 Alamy Stock Photo:** Mike Read (br). **Dreamstime.com:** Ene (cl); Isselee (cl/Parrots, cr); Mikelane45 (tc). **iStockphoto.com:** Utopia_88 (b). **59 123RF.com:** Oleksiy (c). **Alamy Stock Photo:** National Geographic Image Collection (cr). **Dreamstime.com:** Shawn Hempel (br). **Getty Images:** Whitworth Images (tc). **iStockphoto.com:** paulafrench (b). **60 Dreamstime.com:** Martinmark (bl). **61 Dreamstime.com:** Bruce Macqueen (tr). **62 Dreamstime.com:** Rinus Baak / Rinusbaak (tl)

Cover images: Front: 123RF.com: Thawat Tanhai cr/ (Kingfisher); **Alamy Stock Photo:** Ger Bosma l; **Dreamstime.com:** Eng101 ca, Shawn Hempel cra, Korakot Khayankarnnavee cr, Kotomiti_okuma tr, Rinus Baak / Rinusbaak tl; *Back:* **123RF.com:** kajornyot tr; **Dreamstime.com:** Steve Byland bl; **Fotolia:** Stefan Zeitz / Lux tl; **Getty Images:** Rolf Muller cr; *Spine:* **Dreamstime.com:** Kotomiti_okuma b; *Front Flap:* **123RF.com:** Berangere Duforets ca, Ross Taylor br; **Dorling Kindersley:** Natural History Museum, London crb; **Dreamstime.com:** Akinshin bl/ (1), Steve Byland cra/ (1), Donyanedomam br/ (1), Brian Kushner tr, Bruce Macqueen cr, PeterWaters cl, Sergei Razvodovskij cla/ (1); **iStockphoto.com:** DaddyBit cb; *Back Flap:* **NASA:** clb

All other images © Dorling Kindersley
For further information see:
www.dkimages.com

My Findout facts:

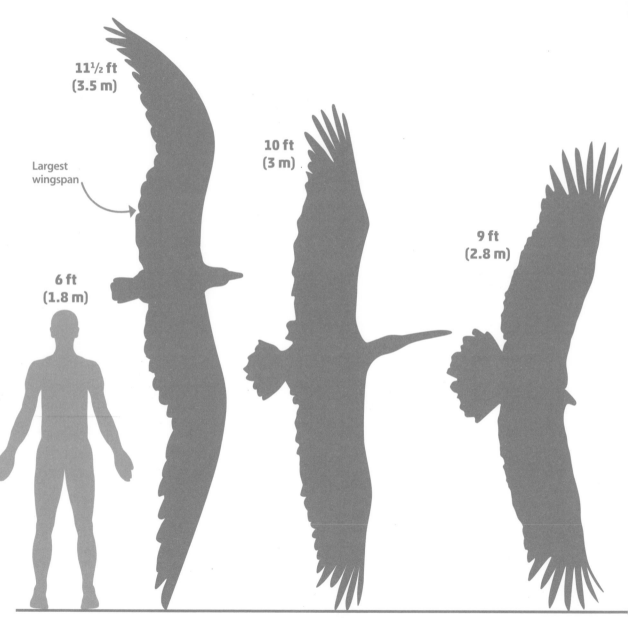

Wingspans

11½ ft (3.5 m)

Largest wingspan

10 ft (3 m)

6 ft (1.8 m)

9 ft (2.8 m)

Human
Like birds, humans walk on two legs. However, we have arms instead of wings.

Wandering albatross
Huge wings let the albatross glide for hours on ocean winds.

American white pelican
In flight, this pelican beats its wings slowly or glides.

Griffon vulture
This vulture soars in the sky on broad wings, looking out for carcasses to feed on.